BUILD A HOST AGENCY

Increase Your Profits
With Ease

Your guide to beginning a simple host agency inside your existing travel agency

By Sharon Emerson, CTC, ECC

http://buildahostagency.com
info@buildahostagency.com

MY BEGINNING.

After working in a brick and mortar agency for 10 years, I moved my office home. Home-based agencies were still quite new and host agencies were just getting started. After the airlines cut the commissions they paid to travel agencies, many agency owners who had depended on these either closed their agencies and retired or moved home. This left scores of agents who had worked in agencies adrift with no way to book travel. This is when the "host" agency concept began to appear.

I had not intended to be a host, but one friend who lost her agency asked if she could come under me. I knew she was a good agent, so I said "sure", not even realizing what that would mean to me in terms of increased revenue. Now, many years later, all of these agent's sales make up over 60% of my agency's revenue.

I had also thought I only wanted local agents that I knew, liked and trusted. But as potential agents came to my school, and after finishing asked if they could join me, I began to be spread out over many states. I am still very picky about who I bring on. I have declined several. One conversation on the phone or one email request can tell me a lot about the quality of the person asking to come on board. Professionalism is very important in this business to be successful. I am not interested in those just wanting to book their own travel. Now I am excited to help you into this new world

WHAT IS A HOST AGENCY?

This is a "home base" for Independent Contractor travel agents. They operate under the host's name for booking with suppliers. They use the host's IATA/CLIA number and the host's phone number. There are no industry standards to become a "host agency". However, an overall knowledge of the what, why and how of the entire industry makes you a better mentor for these Independent Contractors. These are NOT employees and you cannot control what they do as far as times they work, how they get clients, nor where they work from.

WHY BE A HOST AGENCY?

First and foremost you must have a desire to train others with what you know. Without that, you will burn out quickly from the intensity of the host position. By that I mean you are on call for their questions, getting their commission checks and paying them. You also need to be monitoring them to make sure they are working legally as far as licensing requirements are concerned. Second is the additional income that will be generated by these Independent Contractors to increase your bottom line.

BEFORE BECOMING A HOST AGENCY

You must be set up as a Professional Travel Agency. You will need to have the local licensing required for your business in your state and locale. In addition to the local licensing, you will need Seller of Travel licenses in other states, where you have clients, that require this. You also need to have an account with one or more travel insurance companies. There are some states that require a special license to be able to sell insurance in their states. The travel insurance companies can tell you how to do that. Make very sure your E & O insurance will cover your Independent Contractors. Have your travel agency requirements in place such as IATAN/CLIA affiliation needed for booking any travel sale. NACTA and ASTA are organizations that I highly recommend. All of these make you a legitimate travel agency in the eyes of the industry and the government.

In addition to all of the above, you need to have accounts properly set up with the cruise lines, tour operators and other travel suppliers. These will allow you to add other agents to your profiles. There are scores of different companies, but pick some of the most used ones.

As you go along, you can add more. It is best to not spread out your bookings to too many doing the same destinations. You be in charge of who you use based on the service you get from both your representative and inside sales team. There may be a need to switch, but don't spread around the "wealth" of your bookings. Then when you need help, your reps will be there for you. I keep a list of the logins and passwords for all of the suppliers that I set up for each Independent Contractor. But many times the Independent Contractor sets themselves up with certain suppliers and

I let them keep track of those themselves.

WHERE TO FIND AGENTS?

There is nothing wrong with being picky about who you bring on. You want someone with integrity and character. It is better if you have known them on a personal level, but not totally necessary. I find that those retiring by force or by choice from another profession know what it means to start a new profession and how to work to build their new business.

Avoid anyone who thinks being a travel agent means you travel for free. Some think it is a "fun" business to be a travel agent. I hear it all the time. It is "enjoyable", but it is a very serious business dealing with other's dreams and money. It is 24/7/360 and you must be ready to move on something quickly and with a smile. You are still working with "people" and that can be difficult.

If at any point personalities clash, don't be afraid to either talk about it or cut them lose. We don't do the "blame game". They should step up and take responsibility for their mistakes and pay for them, if necessary. They need to be treating your suppliers with professionalism. If at any time I hear that my IC's have been disrespectful to a supplier, I check out the issue. I have worked in agencies where the agents feel they need to yell and belittle the reps. I never tolerate that. Those reps or inside order takers are not our enemies. Sometimes they have to abide by rules that they didn't make. If there is an issue, it is good for you to get involved and try to solve it. Your company is being represented.

There is no "rule" about taking on local vs. non-local agents. These days with technology it is easy to have non-local agents. You can use join.me to see each other's screen or GoToMeeting to have a group meeting. Just make sure they are in touch with their local NACTA or ASTA chapter and get to know their local reps. Also, make certain that they know when there are trade shows, conferences, road shows, and ship inspections that they could go to. I have agents who fly to Seattle for my home-training meetings. Serious agents will make anything work

I have a few agents I have carried for a number of years who book very little. They love the industry and even know quite a lot, but because of financial issues have not been able to work full time. But I consider them "my agents". Now, one of these has come to a point in her life where she is ready to go full time and fulfill her dream. She is getting everything set up to be seriously selling. She even has some clients lined up. It was worth it to keep her in the loop and sending her information. On occasion she came to a seminar or NACTA meeting and in her heart was a travel agent. And now she is. Use your own judgment on each person.

It is good if they have an income to carry them until they can get their business flowing. Many think they will be getting paid right away making lots of money. Here are some possible contacts:

Former agents wanting to come back but not start their own agencies.

These people are so very valuable. They have a wealth of knowledge. The caution I would say is that they may not be flexible about doing business your way. You need to set the rules and if they don't want to follow them, let them go. If they have been gone for a number of years, they may need some training to bring them up to speed with any changes.

Agents from closed agencies or downsized.

These agents may have a variety of years in the business. It maybe good for them to get some current training. If they haven't been on any trips, encourage them to take some FAM trips to become a better agent. Always bring them on with the understanding if they don't fit, you can ask them to leave. If they have been a salaried agent, they may have a problem converting to a commissioned agent. If you can get their sales for the past year, you may be able to show them that being on commission is more lucrative, even though they may have to wait for their commissions until the client's trips are complete.

Newbies.
These definitely need a lot of training and hand holding. Send them to school at http://certifiedtravelteacher.com/agent-training. Make sure they understand what you are requiring of them in productivity. They may have a full time job and wanting to begin exploring the travel industry. It is up to you whether that is OK. I have several like that and that is fine. At some point they will build a data base and be more

productive – or maybe not and they will fall out.

CONTRACT

Written and signed
I use Attorney Jeff Miller's contract form with modifications. What I changed was the commission structure.

Commission split is important to state in the contract.
I have 2 contracts. One for 80/20 for professional agents and one 50/50 for new agents. Make sure the new agent understands at what point you will boost them to 80/20. Maybe based on

productivity or on knowledge. Each case will be different. Will you be splitting the overrides or bonuses from the suppliers? How about the professional fees the agents collect?

Who is responsible for what is important to clarify.
Are you providing leads? Equipment? Payment for advertising materials? Who pays for FAM trips or membership dues?

AFFILIATION WITH YOU

Difference between employee and independent contractor.

This is a legal issue and since I am not an attorney, I will just give you my information. I highly suggest you do not hire employees, unless you need a bookkeeper or receptionist. But the seller of travel must be on commission. They will be way more productive if they have to earn their pay. This is what makes them an Independent Contractor – you do not deduct taxes, you do not have requirements such as hours, or responsibilities.

Putting your information on business cards and invoices, etc.

If the agent wants their own business name, they need to show "Independent

Agent for XYZ. Corporate office 12345 S. Main St, City, State, Zip". Then they need to make sure they have proper licensing for the state they live in, if required. I suggest they talk to their attorney and/or accountant.

If they use your name, it needs to show in small fonts "Corporate Office 12345 S. Main St, City, State and Zip". But use their phone number and address.

The only thing you get from their bookings is the commission check which you should split and send out immediately. The agent gets all confirmations and documents, if there are any. There are still a number of suppliers who only send confirmations to the agency email. In that case, I forward them to the agent as soon as possible.

It is good to put their picture on their business card. Realtors do it and then people remember you. Leave the back blank and not shiny for notes when they swap and drop.

W9 for each agent.
Check with your accountant for their requirements.

E & O Insurance covered in your policy with Berkley Care.

You can cover many Independent Contractors on your policy. But if you get a "huge" number, per Berkely, then you have to ask them what to do. Other companies may have different requirements. Check with who you have now. I don't ask the IC's to pay for E & O insurance. Some hosts may.

COSTS FOR SETTING UP A HOST AGENCY?

At the beginning, there aren't any additional costs.

HOW MUCH TIME IS REQUIRED?

This is all going to depend on each agent you bring on. For all of them, at first you will need to get them set up with the suppliers. The cruise lines are the major ones. After that, I set them up as needed. I have a list of agency information I give to each agent. This has my IATAN #, EIN #, UBI #, WST and CST #s, as well as logins for a multitude of suppliers on their websites. This beginning step takes a little while. After that I don't spend much time except for cutting their commission checks. Every day I forward emails that I think they might want to see, but I screen them. At some point they will each begin getting their own messages. The newer agents will need help deciding on suppliers for every possible booking. So a bit of direction from you will be needed. Then, for every agent you will need to explain your agency's invoice policies. I cover that in my school, but they need to know your methods.

PREFERRED SUPPLIERS

The suppliers on the above mentioned list continues to evolve as we add or delete suppliers. If the agent has been in the business a long time, they may have their own preferences. I do not have a "preferred" supplier list. I feel it is better to use the ones that fit each situation. However, I caution the agents that we don't jump around unless there is a serious issue. The more loyalty to a supplier, the more apt they are to be there when we need help.

FINANCIAL INFORMATION

I have National Transaction Corporation for credit card payments for fees, only. I charge the agent 4% of the fee and then split the balance with them. If they get a check or cash for the fees, they forward it to me and I cut them a check for the split. I have no way of checking to make sure this is happening and that the client isn't giving them the check in their name.

If the agent takes a check for a deposit or final payment, which I discourage, they must forward it to me so I can turn around and send an agency check to the supplier. First, make sure the client's check clears. I require 2 weeks before the due date to get that check turned around.

RESPONSIBILITIES OF EACH

Get their own clients.

Some host agencies provide leads to their agents. However, in my own business I have tried different "lead" programs and I find those putting out the queries are only tire kickers. It is more profitable for the agents to get their own starting with their warm market and moving outward.

Do their own marketing.

This is a topic I very much like to talk about. It could be one reason for you taking on an agent, or not. If they are shy about talking to strangers, then they won't make it in the travel industry. Gone are the days of people walking into a brick and mortar office off the street and booking travel. Home-based agents have to be gently aggressive. I teach 2 classes on marketing as that is how to build a business. As a host, you will have suggestions for what has worked for you, but it is up to each agent to get away from their desks and go after the clients. They may be reticent at first, but they can start with what they know and build from there. If they have never worked from their homes in the past, they may find it hard to settle down and not be "puttering".

Vacation.com has an Engagement program I highly recommend each agent sign up for. They pay for it themselves, but they are linked to my agency and that name is on each piece with the agent's contact info. This is an important way to stay in their client's and prospective client's faces all the time.

Have a link on your website.

I don't find much online booking done on my website, but there are hundreds each month that log onto it for research. Then I get calls for bookings after the clients have researched my site. Passport Online is the only web hosting company that is linked to the consortium Vacation.com and has all their specials of every kind to all parts of the world. Your agents must, at some point, either make their own website and have PPOL put their content on it, or have PPOL do the whole thing. Then it can link to yours. If you are using Fare Buzz for your airline booking engine, that link can also be put on each agent's website. Websites are the way most all travel is being researched these days. Agents are still vital and can sell themselves as the "human" touch for helping clients see the world. They just need to get out of their office and meet the public.

Pay their own telephone and mailing.

Let the agent research and decide the best telephone service for them. If they are going to use a cell phone instead of a land line, they need to check the quality of the service. Many company's service is not clear and as travel agents that is a reflection on the quality of their personal service.

Pay their own fam trips.

The most value an agent can have to a client is to have "been there". The new agents may not be able to afford to travel internationally, but they can certainly take local weekend trips. Encourage them to get out and see the world – at home and abroad. They need to talk with their accountants about deducting their trips as business expenses.

ONGOING TRAINING

My school is for all agents.

It should be imperative that every agent gets foundational training like I offer at http://certifiedtravelteacher.com/agent-training. If you, as a host, sign up as an Affiliate of the program, you will earn 40% commission for each student you send and they will get a 10% discount on the classes. Go to http://cttmembers.com/affiliate to download the free agreement. Taking these classes will take the load of training off your shoulders. After that, they can understand terminology and be a professional asset to you

Local seminars at your home or hotel, etc.

From time to time I invite 3 suppliers to my home along with all my Independent Contractors. I even open my door to many local agents who are hanging by themselves. Often this results in those agents becoming Independent Contractors for me. They are a huge resource because they have probably been in the business for some time and already have a data base, plus lots of wisdom.

I pick suppliers that are different from each other. The meetings start at 10 AM and each supplier gets 1 ½ hour to present. The first one brings a fruit dish, the next one brings lunch and the 3rd one brings cookies!! I have a waiting list of suppliers wanting to come. It always happens that some agents don't know these suppliers and go away becoming clients of the suppliers. I only want suppliers that I or other agents know, like and trust. A win win for everyone.

Now I have added a weekend retreat to a spa resort. The ICs are very excited to get a chance at a short vacation but also to meet each other. We will have a time of sharing our expertise with each other. Just like in the old B & M offices, we can learn from our colleagues.

Require CLIA training.

I feel it is imperative for every agent to begin or continue this training. The classes are valuable whether for cruises or other travel. They may even need to travel some place to take live classes. Valuable ones are when CLIA combines a cruise with training. If you belong to

CLIA, the agents can get a card under you, after they sign up for a class.

Must take FAMS.

I think it is of more value to the agent if they pay their own way. I have a class on FAMS – what they are and how to take them. Having traveled the world on FAM trips, I always sold that destination better when I had seen it.

Must join organizations.

There are many and you, as a host, may have suggestions. I feel NACTA offers the most for the money. There are others such as ASTA, which is now working on the travel industry's behalf inside the federal government. Both of those offer destinational trips at greatly reduced prices. Along with the industry organizations, the agents need to be involved in the communities they live in. This goes along with marketing and meeting prospective clients. Be a "joiner". If that bothers an agent, then they need to get into another industry.

Sending current information.

As the host, you will need to forward emails all day long. It takes a while for agents to get onto the supplier's email lists. Many suppliers will want a list of your agents. But even when you have been an agent for years, you may not get notifications of upcoming seminars and trade shows. If your agents are in another part of the country, you will have to contact their local reps and get them on the list. This is a hard part of an agent belonging to a host who is far away. The reps only know the host and not the agents. I feel it is the host's responsibility to make that known. Your agents may need the rep's help with a booking issue and they need to know each other. I also teach a section on how to work with suppliers. Too many times I have seen agent/supplier conflicts and that is bad for both.

The Travel Institute

has a lot of specialty training that is very valuable. I don't think it is necessary for the agents to get their CTA/CTC certifications. But the DS training is important.

IATAN

It should be a goal for each agent to hit the $5000 commission in order to get their own IATA card. Explain the value of this card as identifying them as a legitimate agent and giving them discounted prices.

KEEPING RECORDS

File systems for each showing supplier, client, total sale, commission. I suggest you have each agent send you a copy of the invoice they are sending their client. Keeping in mind this MUST be done within 3 days of any money being put on the booking. My classes teach how to create invoices and keep files. You may want to require your system with your agents. I set up 2 file folders for each agent – one for invoices they send and one for invoices I have paid commissions on. For the latter one, I attach a copy of the check stub from the supplier. The original check stub goes to the agent with their commission check. I also keep track of my commission earned on a spread sheet showing the sale from the IC for my accountant. You won't need a complicated system unless you are going to build your host agency into many agents. You will find some are selling a lot and some not so much.

Your invoice showing commission payments.

On this invoice I also show the name of the agent, name of the client, name of the supplier, amount of the sale, date, check number and amount of the commission sent to the agent.

Spread sheets for tax purposes.

I have a spread sheet that I copy and send to my accountant at the end of the year. It shows the agent's name, SS #, date, amount of the sale, amount of commission and check #. If you want a more detailed spread sheet, you might want to keep track of the supplier they are selling.

Send commission split as soon as you get the checks.

Never hold their money. I have heard many horror stories about hosts who withhold agent's commissions. It is the agent's responsibility to keep track of their commissions. For new agents you will have to give them guidance on booking hotels and rental cars so they are sure to get commissions, particularly international hotels. Make sure the agents know they should bank their commissions until the trip is over.

What to do when they go away?

The hardest part of being an Independent Contractor is having a backup when you travel. If there are 2 agents close to each other in location and emotion, they can take paperwork to each other when one is gone. However, when both are gone at the same time, it becomes difficult. Without investing in a complex computer system that everyone books with, I have found just having the copy of each invoice for each booking is best. Those invoices must be in detail in case I need to do something for that client while the IC is gone.

For you as the host, you will need a backup. One of my IC's is my backup. That works pretty well. I put all my live files in a basket and take them to her home. She does not have access to my computer but she does have the numbers for my phone to pick up my messages. If I am in a place where I can get cell phone service, I forward my office phone to my cell. I have booked travel all over the world as I am traveling. No one knows where I am!! If you have remote access to your computer and you don't need paperwork, you are probably fine by yourself. I just like a Plan B.

PROFILE FOR POTENTIAL AGENTS

NAME_____

ADDRESS_____

PHONE_____

EMAIL_____

IN TRAVEL NOW: YES_____
NO_____

IF YES, HOW
LONG?_____

WHERE HAVE THEY
WORKED_____

WITH WHOM HAVE THEY BEEN
ASSOCIATED_____

DATA BASE
NUMBERS_____

REASON FOR LEAVING_____

IF NO, WHY DO THEY WANT TO BE IN TRAVEL_____

GOALS_____

PERSONALITY_____

EDUCATION_____

_____

SKILLS_____

_____

_____

_____

BACKGROUND CHECK (HANDLING MONEY)_____

PREVIOUS PROFESSIONS_____

_____

ISBN-10:1482366339
ISBN-13:978-1482366334